A HOW-TO GUIDE: LINKEDIN LEAD GENERATION

2019 Edition

Produced by Lead Cookie

Outbound is simple

Having talked with thousands of business owners over the past few years, our team at Lead Cookie has heard the phrase, "I need more customers and don't know where to start," over and over again.

There's not a lot as frustrating as having a valuable service or product and not having enough people to benefit from it.

Fortunately, for those feeling uncertain where to start, outbound marketing boils down to a comforting simplicity: hitting the right people with the right message at the right time.

And that is *exactly* where any successful campaign starts.

When done correctly, our clients have seen outbound LinkedIn efforts generate . . .

3-8 appointments per month

100-400 new connections per month

Substantially increased LinkedIn traffic

So grab a mug of coffee, settle back into your chair, and learn from our successes (and the mistakes we've made along the way).

250+ campaigns and counting

At the time of writing the 2019 version of this guide, our team is composed of 31 full-time staff spread across three continents.

Our inhouse team of outbound experts worked together to create this guide as a way to share what we've learned along the way.

Here are some of the numbers we've got under our belts.

225+ LinkedIn Campaigns

Over 3 Million Messages Sent

500+ Deals Closed

Connecting people is our passion and we've found a way to do that for each and every one of our clients.

This guide is a chance for us to share what we've learned and to ensure that anyone reading it will be approaching LinkedIn in a way that is thoughtful, engaging, and ultimately respectful of your prospects' time.

The million dollar question:

Who does LinkedIn outreach work for?

Before we dive into the nitty gritty, let's take a second to look at what kind of businesses are most likely to succeed most when it comes to LinkedIn outreach.

To date, we've run campaigns for design agencies, SaaS and software development firms, staff augmentation companies, coaches, consultants, and many other B2B service providers. We've targeted hundreds of different titles at as many industries. And what we've seen is the following:

Generalists Fail, Specialists Succeed

In other words, positioning is *everything*. How you present yourself to your target audience can be the major difference between a successful campaign and one that comes up flat.

While results may vary by industry, we found that we've been able to produce solid results for all of our clients that have a well-defined value proposition and a clear idea of who they want to target.

Clear targeting consists of knowing who benefits the most from your service and how much power they have in making a decision. This is where things like industry, company size, title, etc. come into play.

We've broken down some of the different combinations of value propositions and targeting we've seen prove successful in the past.

#1) Strong Value Proposition + Clear Targeting

There is a difference between *hard* and *soft* value propositions. A strong value proposition proves to the prospect that they can't afford to not respond. It is specific and promises a clear outcome.

- ***Reduce cart abandonment by 40%***
- ***Save 24% on office heating***
- ***Reduce IT expenses by 17%***

All of these are examples of strong value propositions that promise a specific outcome to a clearcut problem.

Is it worth 15 minutes of your time to see if you can save a considerable amount on your heating bills? Probably.

One thing you will notice is that none of these value propositions are weighed down by features. Instead, they focus on the value being created.

The goal of a value proposition is to always show a prospect that their future is better with you by their side.

When brought together with clear targeting, the results for campaigns with strong value propositions tend to be fantastic.

#2) Soft Value Proposition + Good Social Proof + Clear Targeting

So what happens when your value proposition is alright, but not quite enough to get people to give you their valuable time? Maybe . . .

- Your branding agency provides a personalized service

- Your CPA firm delivers a seamless experience from start to finish

- Your software development company is proficient in a number of programming languages

While all of these are valuable benefits of working with you in particular, many of these benefits can be realized with 1,000 other service providers.

A high quality service with a personal touch can do an excellent job of driving referrals, but it isn't necessarily the most effective approach when it comes to outbound outreach.

So how do you set yourself apart in a competitive landscape?

You bring in social proof.

Even if your value proposition isn't the most "stop everything and take my money" kind of offer, that doesn't mean you can't show your value by bolstering it with the previous work you have done.

The best social proof you can bring up is well-known companies within the industry you are targeting.

If you are reaching out to a construction company and bringing up the work you did with Apple or Microsoft, it's not going to be as strong as someone well-known in the industry.

Make sure that your social proof is relatable and impressive (if possible).

Social proof can make up for a soft value proposition as a way to open doors.

Here's just one example of a connection request we sent that had some dynamite social proof:

> Hi {FirstName},
>
> Your profile caught my eye while browsing leaders at media companies. Disney, Fox, and Sony are some of our biggest clients, so I thought I would reach out to connect and say hello.
>
> {SoftwareDevelopmentBusiness}
> Elite software development consulting for enterprises

Even though the offer itself (software development) isn't all that interesting, big names can be a great way to catch a prospect's eye.

Not Sure on Value Proposition + Weak Social Proof + Hazy Targeting

Since we've seen two examples of what ingredients make up a successful campaign, it can be disheartening if your value proposition is up in the air. This spirals into making it difficult knowing *exactly* who you benefit most heavily. Or, if you haven't yet worked with any reputable names, how can you get the first few clients onboard?

Answer: the mindset changes. The new goal becomes finding who is the best fit for your services.

The name of the game is research. Come up with your best hypothesis for who benefits most heavily from your service and find 10 people matching that criteria on LinkedIn. Study them.

Learn who they are, how they speak, and what they see as their priorities. Remember, your goal is to always support them in achieving the future they want.

Once you have this information in hand, run a 2-4 week sprint to test out the value prop and see what people are saying. Are you getting lots of engagement? Do people seem interested in pursuing next steps? Are you running into objections?

Take this information and use it to inform your next steps. If you're seeing initial traction from the value proposition and target market you've chosen, double down on that and turn it into a 3 month trial to solidify your findings.

If you haven't seen much traction, try changing up your value proposition a little. If that doesn't work again, look at the individuals you are reaching out to and consider reaching out to a different title, industry, company size, etc.

We run "discovery" campaigns like this all the time at Lead Cookie. Just be patient and look for smoke. When you find it, see if there is a fire there that can help your business grow.

A framework for positioning

Now that we've seen a few of the attributes we tie to successful campaigns, let's look at how to easily convey the value that you provide to potential clients.

Getting your positioning 100% perfect can be difficult. It's based on industry experience, matching your clients' priorities, being succinct, and clearly solving a problem.

But, for those who are testing new markets, channels, or value propositions, taking the time to get the positioning just right might not be a viable option.

For those situations, here is a quick formula that will get you 80% of the way.

I help X do Y through Z

You can plug the following information into the variables in our formula:

X = Your target customer

Y = Benefit or value you bring them

Z = How you do it

Examples:

Lead Cookie - We help B2B sales teams generate leads on Linkedin through done-for-you prospecting.

[Content Allies](#) - We turn consultants into thought leaders through content marketing

The Linkedin Lead Generation Process

In the spirit of keeping things simple, we've broken our whole process into three steps. That means all you need to do is follow these three steps and you'll start to get your business in front of the right eyes.

Without further ado, the Lead Cookie process . . .

1. **Optimize** - Show your value

2. **Engage** - Reach the right people

3. **Convert** - Engage, re-engage, and then engage once more

1) Optimize

Features fail, values sell

When you've got a strong sense of how to present yourself, it's time to put that information in the places your prospects will see it. A few of the biggest areas for optimization (and ones that won't take too much time) are your personal LinkedIn profile page, your LinkedIn tagline, and your profile picture.

Now keep in mind, optimization is a painful process. It means that you need to check your ego at the door because *this is not about you*.

Instead, it is all about your prospects. The people that you are reaching out to have their own goals and priorities. You better be willing to show them that you understand this . . . and then convince them that you are the best person to get them to where they want to be.

In order to properly position yourself, you might need to decondition yourself a bit. We are constantly battered with the idea that "new is better." But in reality, new is only better if it gets us where want to go in a faster/more efficient/easier way.

Features are a vehicle to carry value, not the value itself

At first, it can be difficult to distinguish values from features. But once you start to see the distinction, it becomes obvious which is more impactful.

- Features: We built X, Y, Z

- Value: We help you make more money/save time/find freedom through X, Y, Z

The more specific you can get with this information, the more successful your campaign is likely to be. If you can throw in metrics to support your claims, even better!

One of the best ways we have found to position yourself in line with your prospect's goals is to visit their LinkedIn profiles. Open up 10-20 profiles of people who match your exact criteria and see what they have in common.

Are they using similar language?

Are they describing similar problems?

Use their own language as a way to position yourself as the solution.

Now that we have a sense of how to position ourselves, we need to put this information somewhere that our prospects are likely to see it.

Optimize Your LinkedIn Profile

#1 - The Tagline

The tagline is the first thing your prospects will see. Your first impression better be a good one.

And you better believe this little guy is everywhere . . .

- When you post in the news feed, the tagline shows up

- When you first land on someone's profile page, the tagline shows up

- When someone sees your message in their inbox, the tagline shows up

- When you are browsing the people who have viewed your profile, the tagline shows up

- When you show up in "Recommended People," the tagline shows up.

For example, here is the LinkedIn profile of one of our inhouse account strategists. Take note of his tagline, as it is the first thing you see when you land on his LinkedIn profile.

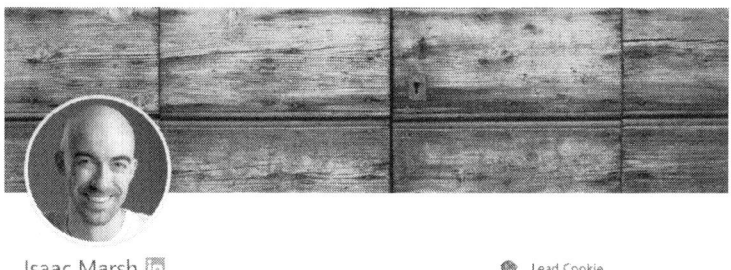

Your tagline is all over LinkedIn and is your chance to hook your prospect's attention, ultimately leading them visiting your profile.

That's the value of a good tagline. It will be relevant, valuable, and memorable.

But not every tagline is going to be good. Instead, the majority of taglines you see on LinkedIn are going to look more like this . . .

- CEO at Company #4905389

- Entrepreneur and Founder of XYZ Co

And that might be fine when everybody knows who you are. But for the majority of outbound, you're going to making new connections with people who don't know you from Adam.

That, unfortunately, means they have no vested interest in your role, your company, or your history because you haven't yet shown how that can help them.

All of your outreach needs to keep in mind that your goal is to support your clients.

Use the tagline to do just that.

#2 - Your LinkedIn Profile

Chances are you've come across someone's LinkedIn page and seen that they wrote an entire novel in the bio section. It's then likely that you decided it was *way too much text* and skipped right over it.

We've been there.

The goal of your LinkedIn profile to your tagline in that you need to convince people that you are the solution to their problems. But this time, you have more than a single line to do so!

The rules of a terrific LinkedIn profile

- *It is all about your prospects*
- *It is clear and concise*
- *It delivers true value*
- *It sets you up as the solution to their problems*

Obviously this takes some time and careful revising to get just right. But after running so many campaigns, we found that the following framework is an easy way to convey this information:

- *What I do (2 sentences on the value you provide)*
- *How I do it (a quick look at your process/features/offer)*
- *Who I work with (a quick explanation on the types of businesses/industries you serve)*
- *What people are saying (client testimonials)*
- *My background (why people should trust you)*

- **Contact Me**

To show this approach in action, we'll use one of our Lead Cookie team member's LinkedIn profile page.

WHAT I DO:

I help B2B companies fill their pipelines with more sales-ready opportunities.

By using LinkedIn connections as a lead-generation channel, we help your team reach new audiences and close more deals. The end result is that you get to focus on making the sale instead of finding it.

HOW I DO IT:

Our team of outbound experts creates targeted messages to speak to your audience. We then reach out and engage your audience using LinkedIn.

Your network grows larger while sales-ready opportunities are delivered to you directly.

WHO I WORK WITH:

Having worked with high-growth teams across many industries, Lead Cookie focuses on B2B businesses looking to grow their client and customer-bases.

WHAT PEOPLE ARE SAYING:

"Lead Cookie has become the most consistent and significant source of marketing qualified leads that we have. I've been amazed at the organization of the service. It is totally worth it and well justified. We have gotten several large, high-level opportunities as well."

Chris Sears, Director of Sales Development and Lead Generation at hc1

MY BACKGROUND:

Having been born with a pen in hand, writing is in my blood. Award-winning ghost writer turned outbound sales specialist.

Stories drive me, so looking forward to hearing more about yours!

CONTACT ME:

Feel free to contact me directly at isaac@leadcookie.com or by connecting with me here on LinkedIn.

#3 - Your LinkedIn Picture

This section is short and sweet. Model your LinkedIn profile picture on the kind of pictures your prospects have. It's a little step that can boost connections when people can relate to you from the very beginning.

While this may seem nuance, it makes a difference.

Our CEO recently tested this in practice. At first he was running an outreach campaign with a headshot he had used for years which consisted of him in a collared shirt. He did a new photoshoot which included him wearing a blazer.

The results were an immediate spike in the number of leads and phone calls booked from the outreach.

The reality is that people will judge you based on your appearance so get a professional headshot to increase your conversion.

That wraps up our section on optimizing your current profile to make sure you are conveying clear value.

Now that we are confident with how we present ourselves to our prospects, it's time to actually engage with them!

2) Engage

The mission of LinkedIn outreach is to start someone along your sales process. Where our clients have seen the most success in the past is when they think of LinkedIn as the conversation starter. It's not a place to ask for something big (even 30 minutes of your prospect's time is going to be valuable).

It's not a place to tell someone every single feature your service or product has.

It's not even that great of a place to drop a thousand values.

Instead, it's a good place to just start things simply in a way that can lead to more detailed conversations down the road.

Once a prospect has raised their hand, it's important to have an idea of where you want to take them.

Is the next step to go grab a coffee? How about jumping on a quick call? Maybe just send over some resources to establish you as a valuable partner.

Think of what your desired outcome is and create at least a basic idea of a sales process or system so that you confidently move people from one step to the next.

And remember, what you are asking of a prospect needs to be reasonable!

Targeting

Engagement starts with reaching out to the right people. Now that we have our message clearly tailored for the audience we want to engage with, it's time to find them.

The best way to be able to build a very clear list of people who match your ideal criteria is to get LinkedIn Sales Navigator. This opens up a huge amount of search criteria that the standard LinkedIn service doesn't have.

So, once you have LinkedIn Sales Navigator, it's time to build out a list of your target accounts or individuals.

There are two ways to do this: account search & lead search.

Lead Search:

Our CEO, Jake Jorgovan, put together a video explaining how to use Boolean filters in the Linkedin Sales Navigator Lead search.

Search "How to use Sales Navigator Account Search to ID Ideal Companies and leads!" on Youtube to find the video.

Account Search:

One of our inhouse account strategists, Rick Williams, put together a video explaining the best way to ID companies matching your ideal criteria. Feel free to check out the video here:

Search "How to use Sales Navigator Account Search to ID Ideal companies and leads" on Google to find video.

--

Now there is one thing to keep in mind about LinkedIn searches: they give a lot of power to filter by specific criteria . . . but they can be lacking when it comes to demographic and psychographic targeting.

For example, you can't filter by age, gender, etc.

You can't filter by intent or specific behavior patterns.

But don't despair! These filters are powerful when used correctly. You can filter by keywords, technology stacks, and even specific LinkedIn groups.

And, you can also choose what you *don't* want to target!

For the targeting that you can't find LinkedIn filters for, you'll often need to do a second round of verification (we do this for certain accounts and refer to it as "hand-qualifying").

Depending on how strict your criteria is for your ideal client, this extra qualification process can be very valuable in letting you ensure your message is targeted.

Starting conversations

The prep work we've looked at so far is the necessary foundation for the outreach.

Now that we know who we are reaching out to and how we want to position ourselves, we can start sending messages that are relevant and valuable.

The outbound process that has shown itself to drive the most results is fairly simple . . .

- Step #1: Send Connection Requests
- Step #2: Drip Messages Over Time

Let's break each of these steps down.

Step #1: Send Connection Requests

There are a few major things to keep in mind when sending connection requests.

1) It can feel a bit strange at first to be sending connection requests to people you might not know. However, that is *exactly* what LinkedIn was designed for, so send away!

2) At the time of this publication, you can send a maximum of 75 connection requests per day. There is also a limit of 750 outgoing connection requests at a time. If you hit this limit, you can remove some

prospects from your queue and send to new ones.

3) Ramp up slowly. If you go from sending a connection request every few days to 50 in a day, you can flag LinkedIn's security measures. Start with 5 the first day, 10 the next, 20 after, and keep bumping up til you hit 75.

4) We **do not recommend** using automation tools for connection requests. Not only is it against LinkedIn's terms of service, but these tools don't do a good job of filtering good leads from bad ones.

Now that those few key points are out of the way, let's take a look at the actual connection process.

You want it to be natural and you want to give a reason for reaching out. This can be as simple as mentioning a common industry, job title, or change in companies.

Second, you want the connection request to be very conversational. It's a 300 character limit, so make it short, sweet, and a solid foundation to build on.

Message 1 - The Connection Request

Hi {FirstName},

Saw that you're focused on {Industry} and I wanted to reach out to connect. Would love to hear what you're working on!

{Me}
I help {Industry} companies do {XYZ}

Notice how this message has zero sales pitch in it.

Instead, all we do is add the tagline under our name as a way to get the value that we provide across without a full-on pitch. Instead, we are saying, "I did my homework."

The second thing you will not is the very minimal usage of the word "I". This is because the outgoing request should be about the prospect, not you.

This entire approach can be summarized in a great quote from the sales legend Jeffrey Gitomer.
"People don't like being sold, but they love to buy."

This approach puts you in front of your ideal prospects and positions you in a way where they have the option to say yes or no. It's not salesy, and not pushy and as a result, people come to you.

Step #2: Drip Messages Over Time

Please note: we have added a number of example frameworks at the very end of this book. Please see the "Additional Resources" section for more information.

Message 2 - The Value Hammer

Once someone has accepted your connection request, it's time to drop the value hammer. In other words, thank them for accepting the request and then show them where you can take them.

Again, it can't be stressed enough: a good value proposition situates you as the enabler of their vision. If you don't know who your ideal client is or what they care about, your outreach just isn't going to work.

But when you do have this information in hand, you can write an absolute knockout of a value message.

There are more than a few ways to structure these messages, but they should be no longer than 5 sentences. You can use the first two for thanking them and laying a foundation.

The next paragraph should hammer home what you've done in the past and why you are the best person to help them in their ultimate pursuit of life, love, and liberty . . . or maybe just show how you can make them more money.

Finally, the last sentence should be a very clear directive for next steps. In other words, the call to action. However, please note that you still need to be cautious of coming across as too salesy. So, to avoid this sales-trap, make the call to action about continuing the conversations as a dialogue, not a one-way pitch.

For this example, we'll take a QA testing software targeting health institutions . . .

> *Hey {FirstName}, thanks for connecting. Was curious, is QA testing a bottle-neck in your development process?*
>
> *Many of our customers, like the National Institute of Health, came to us looking to automate their regression QA testing in a scalable way. Using our low-code tool, they've been able to make their testing agile.*

> Would be interested to hear what you're doing to make your QA testing more efficient.

As you can see, the first two sentences are just a casual thanks that is followed up with a quick question. The goal is to engage the prospect and have them hooked with a pain-point we know they are likely to have.

After that, we can slip in one of our biggest customers and share how they were able to overcome that pain-point. Only after we have shown ourselves to know our prospect's problems and show some credibility, do we say how we do it. Features come after values.

Finally, we put in a very casual call to action: if you're currently tackling this pain-point, I'd love to hear how.

The ball is in their court. It's relatively pressure-free and shows respect.

In addition, sometimes it is worth testing out a shorter message to just get the conversation started.

See the following example:

> Hi {FirstName}, great to connect. My firm helps consultants establish themselves as industry thought leaders through content marketing. Would you be interested in learning more?

It's short, it's simple, and again it puts the ball in our prospect's court. We're being courteous and respectful of their answer.

At the end of the day, there are many different ways that you can approach the value message. Try a few (we've added a few more in the additional resources section at the end of this eBook), and see which one gets the best results.

Message 3 - Want to See More?

If you haven't heard back from a prospect after a week or so of sending the value hammer, it's time to show a bit more credibility.

The third message is a *perfect* place to try to engage your prospects in one of two ways:

1) Include a client testimonial while reframing the pain-point

    or

2) Ask if they want to see a case study or share a valuable resource

If you're going with #2 and wanting to share a case study, it's very important that you simply ***ask*** if the prospect wants to see it. Do not assume they do and send a link.

We have seen a whopping 5-7x engagement rate when it comes to asking versus sending. Sending a link doesn't encourage your prospect to converse. And that's what we're after.

We'll continue with our low-code QA software as an example of sharing a testimonial and what sharing a case study could look like:

> Hey {FirstName}, working with new vendors can be intimidating. That's why we sit down with our customers when they start using our low-code QA tool to help them establish a suite of tests tailored to their exact needs. Here's what one customer said about us recently...
>
> {TESTIMONIAL}
>
> What tests are you currently relying on when you roll out updates? I'd be happy to have our team recreate them in our tool so you could automate it at scale.

OR

> Hey {FirstName}, recently we helped {TestimonialCompany} speed up their QA testing by 43% in two months.
>
> We put together a case study sharing how we did it. Would you like me to send it to you?

As always, these messages are about your prospect. Show them how you can help them get where they want to go and it will be difficult for them to not respond!

Message 4 - Professional Persistence Meets Classy Goodbyes

The final message in the sequence. We like to send this message 5-7 business days after sending the previous message.

This message has two goals:

1) See if there is a better time to connect

2) Show our prospects we respect their time and space

You can experiment with more messages, but we've settled on a 4-part sequence to deliver value without the risk to your brand that constant messaging can have.

As always, keep it short, sweet, and simple.

> Hey {FirstName},
>
> Having reached out a couple times over the last few weeks to discuss automating your QA regression testing with our low-code tool, I'm going to assume it's not a good time to connect.
>
> Would there be a better time for me to reach out later in Q4, or is there someone else I should be speaking to?
>
> {ME}
> {URL}

Additional frameworks for outreach campaigns:

We've included a list of the frameworks our team at Lead Cookie uses in the appendix section of this book.

Please see it to determine which framework is most likely to produce results for your business.

3) Convert

Now that you've got connection requests sending and messaging frameworks to work with, it's time to run a test campaign. Send connection requests and follow-up messages for 1-3 months, gather the results, and determine if your campaign was a success.

If you're not getting much interest, maybe it's time to check your targeting or your messaging.

If not many people are accepting your connection requests, it might be worth changing up your tagline.

The name of the game is constant testing and revising until you find your sweet spot.

And, if things are going well from the very beginning, don't let that stop you from seeing if you can get even better results!

Moving leads along your sales process

Once responses start piling into your LinkedIn inbox, you might not have a firm idea of how to move them along your sales process.

To help ease these conversations to eventual sales, we put together some of our best tips and tricks.

1) Start conversations

The fundamental difference with this type of LinkedIn outreach from other cold outreach is that the purpose is to start conversations. While most cold outreach is pushing directly for a sale, this form of LinkedIn outreach is instead focused on getting your foot in the door at target accounts.

You aren't making a hard pitch in most of your messages, so as a result, you don't get a hard business response every time.

Instead, you will find that many people engage in a conversation with you. They may ask you a question about your business, what you do, who you serve, and how you can help them.

Or, in some cases, they may just strike up a random conversation about mutual interests or where you live.

This throws some people off who are new to this type of outreach, but in reality, these conversations are where all of the benefits are.

You start talking with someone, build up some trust, and then move it to a sales conversation.

Don't dive into this form of outreach ready to sell, sell, sell. Instead, start with a conversation.

2) Don't try to close a deal on LinkedIn . . . your goal is a call or appointment

One of the biggest mistakes I see people make is that they have someone ask "Tell me more about what you do" and they respond with a breakdown of *everything* they do.

Their answer takes the person through all the details of what they do, and why the prospect should buy.

The result is crickets on the other side . . .

Remember, people like to buy. They don't like to be sold.

Your goal with Linkedin is to just create enough interest and intrigue to move the conversation from Linkedin to a phone call or email dialogue.

Don't try to close the deal on Linkedin.

Instead, try to let the conversation naturally transition to a phone call. That's where you can make the actual sale.

3) Research your prospects before you respond

When you have several unread messages, it's tempting to just fire off a response to each one quickly and be done with it.

But if you really want to see the best possible results, you should take a few minutes to research each prospect and craft a personal response according to what you learn about them.

See the example below for a personalized response:

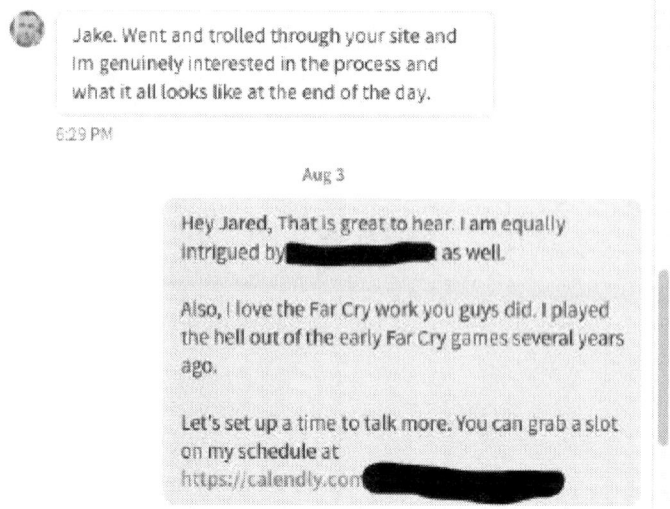

4) Ask questions

One of the fastest ways to kill a Linkedin conversation is to just give someone your pitch and wait for a response.

Instead, what you want to do is ask questions to keep the conversation moving along. And eventually when the conversation is focused on the values you can provide, then ask to transition to a phone call or appointment.

Questions are the foundation of a good conversation.

And a good conversation is how you build trust with your prospects.

Ask questions and talk about your prospect more than you talk about yourself.

Closing Thoughts

Now that we've had a chance to look at the process of generating qualified leads via LinkedIn, let's talk expectations.

On average, our clients see 3-20 qualified leads per month. In some cases, we've seen upwards of 30+ qualified leads in a single month, but this does tend to happen more often for businesses with a strong value proposition and clear targeting.

But, worth keeping in mind, this approach is also likely to generate a lot of leads who simply aren't interested in your offer. Whether it's a matter of bad timing or they simply don't have a need, there will be disinterest.

It's important to keep in mind that Linkedin is a social network, not a database. That means each person gets to self-classify their own profile. It's not uncommon for a one-person consultancy to list themselves as company size of 11-50 just to look bigger than they are.

So keep in mind that some poor fits will slip through now and then, but with good targeting and clear processes to verify contacts are a good fit, you can be sure that the majority of leads coming through are strong candidates for your business.

There is a time investment to all of this though. You're likely looking at ~90 minutes a day to send out connection requests, respond to inbound leads, and filter through the good and bad fits.

We highly recommend hiring a lead generation service or virtual assistant to do a lot of the front-loaded work for you. By removing the work of sending out requests and filtering through qualified and unqualified fits, you can instead spend 15-20 minute per day nurturing the leads that are generated.

High-Quality Leads within 30 days

Depending on your business, you might not see your first deals close within a month. But, if you are consistent with your outreach and have a strong value proposition, you'll see leads entering into your sales pipeline.

That being said, this entire process does take time and energy. That's why we strongly recommend bringing in external help to take care of the front-end work.

Whether this is a VA or an external service provider, the time you save will free you up for having meaningful conversations with the leads generated.

Please feel free to reach out to us at hello@leadcookie.com or LeadCookie.com if you're interested in how our team of outbound experts can jumpstart your lead generation efforts.

As mentioned earlier, the next few pages will include additional resources that can be valuable for your sales positioning and outreach.

We hope that this guide to LinkedIn outreach was valuable; thank you for taking the time to read through!

- The entire Lead Cookie team

Additional Resources

7 Linkedin Outreach Frameworks that generate results

- The Standard
- The Free Resource
- The Portfolio Approach
- The Coffee / Lunch Ask
- The Market Research Approach
- The Direct Pitch
- The Audience Growth Approach

Framework 1: The Standard Approach

The standard approach brings together the different pieces that we looked at throughout the entirety of this eBook. For the majority of us our clients, we've found this to be the most optimal approach.

How the approach works:

Connection Request - Send a short, non-salesy connection request

Message 2 - Send over a thank you message + ask a simple question

Message 3 - Send over an article or piece of content

Message 4 - Make a direct pitch asking for a meeting

Examples of the standard:

Software Development Shop

One great example of the standard is a software development company that specializes in an emerging programming language.

For our second message we ask the question:

> *"Are you currently using {ProgrammingLanguage} and if so what are your thoughts on it?"*

We find that this simple question will get prospects talking and start a technical conversation that can convert into closed deals.

Consulting Firm

We have another consulting firm that specializes in supporting a specific enterprise application. For our outreach, we target key individuals who appear to be using this enterprise application.

We ask the probing question

> *"Are you currently using {Software} and if so, how happy are you with it on a scale of 1-5?"*

This question is easy for the prospects to answer and it gives our consulting firm data on if that client is a good prospect. If the client answers a 4 or below, they can ask *"What would it take to get that to a 5?"*

—

When we started, this was the only approach we ran and it worked pretty well for a good number of clients.

And today it still works great in many situations.

Yet we have also innovated and found that for certain companies or target buyers, the conversations generated weren't converting quite as well as we would have liked.

That is why we have innovated several different approaches.

Framework 2: The free resource offer

One framework that has produced amazing results, even in extremely tough markets, is the free resource offer.

Here is how the framework works:

> **Connection Request -** Light connection request positioning your company
> **Message 2 -** "I put together this free resource. Would you like me to send it to you?"
> **Message 3 -** Reiterate the value of the free resource and offer it again
> **Message 4 -** Direct pitch for a meeting

There is one key thing to understand about this approach.

You don't simply send the free resource to everyone. We find doing that converts extremely poorly.

Instead, you describe your free resource, and then offer it to your target prospects.

This does a few things.

1. It offers value on the front end.
2. It gets their permission before you send anything over.
3. It gets them to that first small yes.

Examples of this approach in action:

Niche Digital Marketing Firm

We have a digital marketing firm that is niched in a specific industry vertical. Our outreach is along the lines of.

> *"We helped {X} company achieve {Result}. We wrote up a case study that shows exactly how we did it. Would you like me to send it to you?"*

The results with this approach are often hundreds of *"Yes, please send it."*

It gets people to that first yes. Not everyone converts to a call, but it takes an extremely challenging market and can produce results.

Offering a book to enterprise buyers

We have another client who specializes in working with high level VP's at Fortune 500 companies. These are big companies that are traditionally very hard to reach.

Yet this client happens to have written a book specifically for this target market.

So we reach out and say . . .

> "I have written a book on X topic. It includes lessons I have learned from working with {name drop 3-4 other Fortune 500 clients}. Would you like me to send you a copy?"

The results from this have been amazing. One client said:

> "Your team has generated me more results and engagement in the past two weeks than I have gotten

with any marketing firm I have hired over the past few years."

The value is offered on the front-end and it caught people's interest. From here, it was easy to move people along the sales process.

Framework 3: The Portfolio Approach

For many creative agencies, copywriters, freelancers, or marketing firms, your portfolio will sell you more than anything else.

At the end of the day, your portfolio is your greatest sales tool. It gives an immediate and credible sense of who you are and what you can achieve.

How this approach works:

> **Message 1 -** Light connection request to position your offer
>
> **Message 2 -** My company does XYZ. Would you like to see our portfolio?

That's it.

Dead simple.

What will happen is you will get responses from many people saying "Sure, please send it over."

And not all of them will have a need right now. But some of them might respond with a project.

And others may file your info aside for future needs.

This works extremely well for any clients who do visual or writing-based work.

Examples of this approach:

Copywriter

We have a niche copywriter who specializes in a particularly tricky segment to write copy for. In our onboarding she said "Once someone sees my portfolio, they are typically amazed and will bring me on for a project whenever it is a right fit."

So we did this outreach to her target market and as a result she has had several high level dream clients responding to her and reviewing her portfolio.

Development Agency

We have another development agency as a client who has a particularly impressive portfolio of work. We reach out to target buyers for their work and offer to showcase their portfolio and as a result they get 5-10 people per day who are looking at and reviewing their portfolio.

It's important to realize that not everyone who looks at your portfolio can and will hire you today.

But each time you show it to someone else, you are making yourself aware to them as a resource, even if it is not now.

Each time someone raises their hand and says "Yes, please send it," you have found another person who may be a buyer either today or someday down the line

Framework 4: The Coffee / Lunch Ask

For clients who specialize in working with local businesses, we have found that the coffee / meeting ask framework performs extremely well.

This tends to work better among small business owners than it does enterprise, but we have still seen results when targeting enterprise accounts.

How this approach works:

Message 1 - Light connection request positioning your offer and showing that you are in the area
Message 2 - Ask them to coffee / lunch and give a reason (Networking, partnerships, to see if you can help them, etc.)
Message 3 - Nudge the coffee ask
Message 4 - Make a lighter pitch for a call or to send over more information

Now, there are challenges with this approach as not every single lead who says yes may end up being a good fit. So you may need to prepare an out if you decide someone is not worth meeting after looking into them a bit further.

But for the most part, this approach can produce some great results and set up plenty of meetings.

Examples of this approach working well:

Videographer

We have a client who specializes in a few key verticals in their local geography. We use this coffee-based outreach to set up meetings. Within weeks he was already sending over quotes for new projects.

Offshore Development Shop

We work with several offshore and nearshore dev shops. Many of these companies will often send someone to the USA or to a target geography to hold sales meetings.

We have used outreach to set them up coffee or lunch meetings during their business trips and visits.

—

When using this approach, make sure you are focusing on a target market that would actually be willing to meet.

Framework 5: The Market Research Approach

For many of our customers, they are trying to launch a new business or validate a new niche.

While an end sale may be the goal, they also need to validate their offer and get feedback from the market.

In these cases, we have found that being authentically transparent about where you are at and what you are trying to learn produces great results.

But please note that you should *never* use this tactic in an inauthentic way. If you try to use this tactic just to get engagement so you can make a sale, without a genuine interest in customer feedback, don't expect stellar results.

Here is how the framework works:

> **Message 1 -** Light connection request describing that you are launching something new
> **Message 2 -** Ask if they would be open to providing feedback

Message 3 - Bump the thread up and ask for additional feedback

Message 4 - Make a more direct pitch about what you are offering them

Examples of this approach:

Software Company

One of our clients offers a software solution for the healthcare industry. Their CEO made a large pivot in their value proposition and the sales team was tasked with capturing market feedback quickly.

We used this market research approach and the team held over 18 calls within the first 45 days.

Not all of these calls were great customer fits, but they each gave them valuable insight and feedback on the market.

Launching a new consultancy

We had another client who had come from working in corporate job positions for his entire career.

For our outreach, we focused on simply asking to hop on a call and gain feedback from his target customers so he could better understand how to serve them.

As a result, over the course of 3 months he held well over 20 calls and had numerous other high-level decision makers responding and offering to help him.

—

If you use this approach, be sure to use it in an authentic way to gain feedback on your new value proposition or offering.

Framework 6: The Audience Growth Approach

For several of our clients, the goal of their outreach is not to generate new leads and sales. Instead, they are seeking to grow their audience and bring more awareness to their content or gain more email subscribers.

For these types of customers, we have found a very simple two-step message sequence works quite well.

How the framework works:

> **Message 1 -** Light connection request saying something like "I regularly publish content for people like yourself, so I wanted to connect."
>
> **Message 2 -** You can see more of the content I am publishing at {Website}. Do you have any topics you would like to see us cover?

This simple approach will create significant awareness among your target audience and give you valuable feedback as to what your target audience actually wants to hear.

This is a simple yet great way to grow your audience and build a community of readers both on your website and on your Linkedin profile.

Examples of this framework:

One of our customers is ManagingEditor.com. This is a website targeted at anyone who manages content for a living.

So for our approach we reach out to their content directors, content producers, content marketers, and many others in this field.

We are not pitching any of them, but simply connecting and making them aware that this new content hub exists.

As a result, our client builds a Linkedin audience of their target customers, drives them to their website, and gains incredible audience feedback at the same time.

Framework 7: The Direct Pitch Framework

You will notice that all 6 frameworks described so far are very non-salesy.

They do not focus on direct pitching but instead focus on other ways to create value or start a conversation.

Now, in some cases these approaches may not actually be the best solution. In some cases, you need to pitch directly.

This tends to work the best when your value proposition and targeting is extremely well refined and tested.

How the framework works:

> **Message 1 -** Light connection request that establishes a common foundation
> **Message 2 -** Pitch your value proposition and ask for meeting
> **Message 3 -** Offer a resource or try another angle

Message 4 - Pitch another angle and ask for a meeting

Examples of when this approach works well:

One instance where this approach worked very well for us was for a very unique offering.

The client offered negotiation services to help customers reduce specific enterprise contract prices.

It was pay-for-performance, and the client could easily help a company save hundreds of thousands of dollars per year just by renegotiating their contracts.

Basically, the value proposition was amazing and it was a very "Blue-Sky Concept."

When we say Blue-Sky, that means it was an offer and a concept that most of the audience had never heard of and they did not know this kind of service existed.

Blue-Sky is essentially the opposite of commoditized.

So for this client, the direct pitch approach worked because the value he offered was so amazing, and because it was performance-based, there was very little downside.

This process should generate results within 30 days

You probably won't close a deal in 30 days, but if you are doing this and have a strong positioning and service to sell, then you should receive leads within 30 days.

Everything I described here is a TON of work. Like we mentioned before you can expect to invest 90 minutes per day if you do this on your own.

But with the support of a VA or through hiring Lead Cookie's done-for-you [Linkedin Lead Generation](#) service, you can get this down to 15-20 minutes of time investment per day.

If you have good positioning and a good product or service, then this tactic will work for you in time.

It's just a matter of committing and sticking to it.

Have you experimented with these tactics or any others on Linkedin? If so send us an email at hello@leadcookie.com

READY TO RAMP UP YOUR LEADS ON LINKEDIN?

Check out **Lead Cookie**. We help B2B companies generate leads on Linkedin via done-for-you prospecting.

Guaranteed high-quality leads in 30 days or your money back.

Learn more and say hello at LeadCookie.com

Printed in Great Britain
by Amazon